Flying over Bournemouth seafront The Royal Air Force Battle of Britain Memorial Flight commemorate the past of the RAF's Air Combat Power - **Lest We Forget.**

1

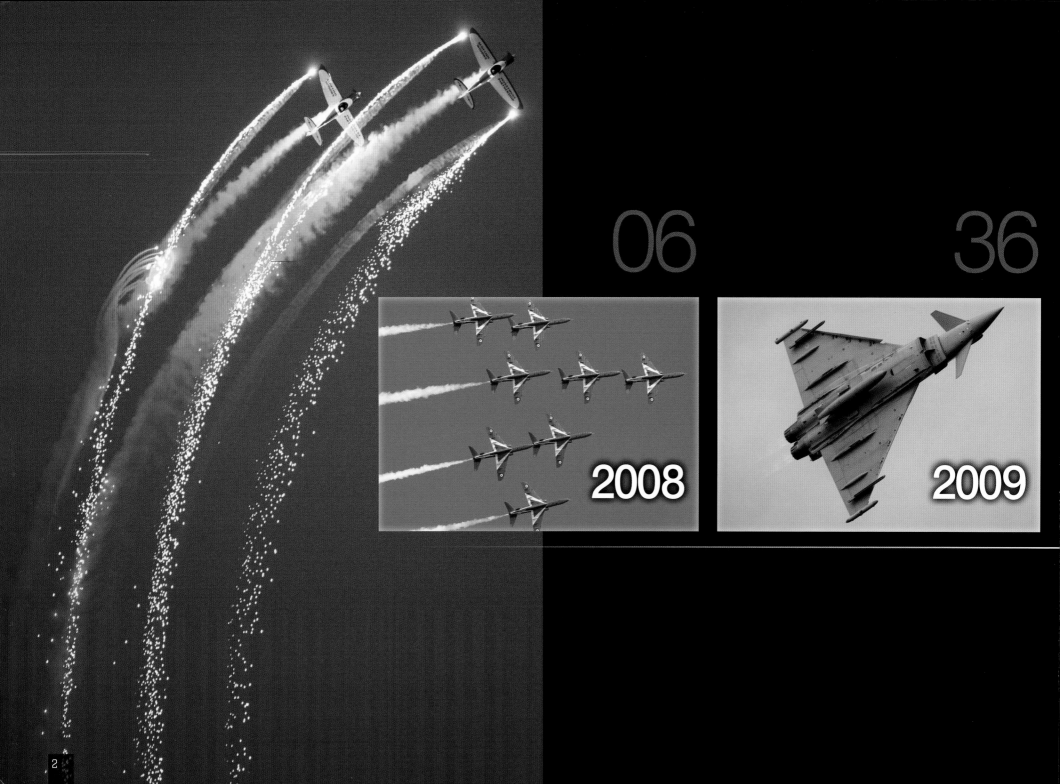

06

36

2008

2009

2

the contents

the foreword

By Jonathon Whaley
Miss Demeanour Hunter Jet pilot

It's great to be back in Bournemouth again this year, for the sixth Air Festival.

Bournemouth's show only began in 2008 and it was a brave step to put on a four day show. The show is now a fully established festival and if you'll excuse the pun, a huge success on many fronts. I can't help feel that those who took that decision, should be looking back with great satisfaction.

For the display pilots, the site doesn't get much better. In fact, if we could turn the country through 180 degrees to make the beach north facing, it would be impossible to make it any better! The airfield is close, so even if the weather is not particularly brilliant, we can often still make it to the display – and we've had most of the extremes of weather in Bournemouth in the last five years.

The display line is nice and long (and always fully packed!) which helps in presenting a good display. There is exceptional viewing for everyone but especially for those up on the cliff top. From there they have a wonderful view of the displays, set against the backdrop of the bay and everything else that goes on there. For those lower down on the piers, we have to resist the temptation to give them a closer encounter! After each day's show, there is an astonishing number of outstanding photographs put up on the web, testaments of the day's action and not just in the air.

Bournemouth Air Festival is extremely popular with pilots and ground crews. We are accommodated in the town with easy access to and from the airfield. This puts us in the middle of everything – we can enjoy not just the flying but get back to the seafront to experience the atmosphere. We are part of the show in the round rather than just flying in and out.

The organisers provide opportunities for people to meet many of the display pilots, ask about them and their planes, collect signatures in programmes and pick up whatever goodies they might be handing out.

When display pilots talk about shows they really like going to, whether it's fun to go there, enjoyable to participate in, or the way we and our ground crews are looked after at the airfield and the show, Bournemouth is up there at the top. But as a complete package Bournemouth is a winner hands-down.

On a personal note, distinctive to Bournemouth, in the days after the show, I (or more truthfully "Miss Demeanour") receive paintings and drawings from children of all ages, sent by their teachers or parents. In return, I send them Miss Demeanour stickers.

Flying the display, we lack crowd interaction. The closest I get is my fly-by with the canopy open, waving and seeing the crowd wave back. To receive drawings and paintings,

especially from children who have taken such care over their pictures and the trouble taken by parents and teachers to track down my address, is very touching.

The majority of people watching the displays might never think of going to an airfield based show.

Bournemouth is not just an air show but four full on days and nights of buzzing festival atmosphere. There's so much to do, it's no surprise that it attracts so many people. Still, somehow we aircrew still manage to find one of the many great restaurants that can squeeze us in at short notice!

In the air, on the land and on the sea, there really is something for everyone.

Enjoy the show.

the sponsor

By Bryan Callow
Managing Partner

Fish and chips, sunshine, sand, septuagenarians. Bournemouth beach has it all.

But every August it comes alive with the sound of music to we who never grew up. The Hawk, the Hunter, the Typhoon and the Tornado. The Spitfire, the Lancaster, the Hurricane and, with luck, the mighty Vulcan. There is poetry in the air even before the engines start up.

And then there are the Red Arrows. Their dedication, bravery and teamwork has become a metaphor for all that is great about Great Britain. You know they're coming but it still catches you by surprise as the ground shakes and they roar over the cliff-top. It's over all too soon but the photographs linger on.

This amazing book contains the best of the pictures captured during the first five years of the Bournemouth Air Festival. It captures it all. The drama, the excitement, the jaw-dropping precision of the displays surrounded by the fun and music and humour of the side-shows.

Castle Cameras are proud to have been asked to sponsor this souvenir book. The photographs are an inspiration. Enjoy it and pass it on.

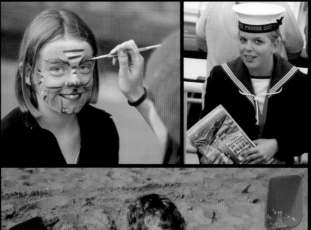

2008

2008

The skies were a bit cloudy, but the first Bournemouth Air Festival kicked off in style on Thursday, August 28, 2008. After several years of planning, it was time to take to the skies with an ambitious four-day event. Civic chiefs were expecting up to one million visitors and projected that the boost to the economy would be around £17 million.

After two-and-a-half years of planning, showgoers were treated to a host of flying, including the raucous Eurofighter Typhoon, Battle of Britain Memorial Flight, Sea Vixen, the Wingwalkers, Black Cats, Chinook, Yakovlevs, Sea Hawk, Catalina, Folland Gnat and, of course, the mighty Red Arrows.

Away from the skies, there was plenty to do on the ground, with the armed forces present in numbers and a balloon glow in the gardens.

There were few disappointments, although the Cold War Vulcan jet – a huge crowd-puller, had last-minute technical issues and could not perform.

Crowds over the weekend were estimated at around 750,000, with 380,000 attending on the Saturday alone. The public, council, sponsors and pilots all sang the praises of the inaugural event.

All in all, the first festival was a big success and organisers promised that it would be back bigger and even better in 2009.

The Russians are coming! The daredevil aerobatics of the Yakovlevs and (right) the Red Arrows with one of their stunning formations.

The elegant American-built Catalina, a flying boat of the 1930s and 1940s and the most successful aircraft of its kind.

The British Eagle Douglas DC6, (far left) once a familiar sight at UK airports at the beginning of the package holiday boom in the 60s. Pilots and ground crew from the Blue Eagles (top left) and gardener Steve Rowland with a RAF tribute flower bed (bottom left). The mighty Chinook (above).

Three images of the beautiful and iconic Lancaster bomber, always one of the show's most popular and evocative aircraft.

Accompanied (above) by the Spitfire and Hurricane, making up the historic Battle of Britain Memorial Flight.

One of the most memorable images of the Air Festival, as the Red Arrows roar in over the town, watched by people with a superb rooftop vantage point.

Hot air balloons provided some of the most spectacular sights of the festival as Bournemouth Gardens was illuminated by the Balloon Glow. Night Air has become one of the most important and popular elements of the whole event.

The Blue Eagles display team (above and right) and just some of the hundreds of boats that drop anchor in the bay to get a great view.

The Eurofighter, (far right) better known as the Typhoon, is the noisiest of the participants with its ear-splitting roar.

Clockwise, inside the Royal Fleet Auxiliary Mounts Bay, the Typhoon, the historic Catalina, Mounts Bay and a landing craft ferrying passengers to and from the pier.

The Gnat T1, still wowing the crowds, years after it stopped being the fast jet used by the Red Arrows. It has seen service all over the world, including Finland, India and Yugoslavia.

The Guinot Wingwalkers (left) produce another display of daring and skill with stunts that would give most of us nightmares. The Battle of Britain Memorial Flight's Hurricane (top) and the four-strong team of Yaks (below)

Crowds flock to the beach and cram onto the pier to make sure they are within touching distance of displays and can soak up the atmosphere, while members of the Air Training Corps also enjoy a bird's eye view. The Blades (right) go through their paces with aircraft just feet apart at various points.

The De Havilland Sea Vixen is a local legend having been lovingly restored at Bournemouth. She is only airworthy example of her kind in the world and is the fastest privately owned jet in Europe.

Five of the nine Red Arrows streak across the seafront, smoke on, as the crowds watch from the beaches, clifftop and a flotilla of boats. The picture was taken from the vessel Mounts Bay.

The Blades break for one of their most thrilling routines in front of the crowds on the packed beach (left). Flying more sedately is the Piper Pawnee (below) and bottom, the Battle of Britain Memorial Flight of Lancaster, Hurricane and Spitfire.

Trailing smoke behind them, members of the RAF Falcons display team parachute are watched by onlookers. The Falcons are widely recognised as the UK's premier military parachute display team.

The Lynx (far left), the thrilling Yakovlevs (left), four of the nine Red Arrows (top), and the versatile Typhoon Eurofighter (above), always one of the biggest draws at the Air Festival.

The Guinot Wingwalkers and their gravity-defying stunts (far left), the Red Arrows in full formation (left). A stunning image of the Sea Vixen (above) banking over a flotilla of boats.

DAILY ECHO

OFF TO A FLYER!

SKY'S THE LIMIT: RAF Battle of Britain Memorial Flight's Spitfire flies over Poole Bay, with the Purbeck hills in the background
ID: 7261682

By Julie Magee
julie.magee@bournemouthecho.co.uk

BOURNEMOUTH'S first air festival took off in style yesterday with stunning displays in cloudy skies between the two piers.

Civic chiefs hope that up to one million visitors will flock to the town for the four-day event and boost the local economy by an estimated £17.5 million.

Those wanting a guaranteed "front seat" on the cliff-top to view the breathtaking aerial action were prepared to pay a premium for a night's bed and breakfast accommodation in a sea view room.

The borough's head of tourism Mark Smith pledged that the air show was just the first of many. "It's taken two-and-a-half years of planning but it's absolutely amazing.

"Now we've got a world class event and the right formula, we will be making the air festival an annual attraction at the end of August. The date each year will be determined by the bank holiday.

"The setting, between the piers, is perfect. Times are tough but it's a free event for families, not just from outside the area but local residents. There's so much for them to do, even if the sun isn't shining."

Kevin Wood, director of the Cumberland Hotel on the East Cliff, said sea view rooms had been snapped up weeks ago with guests paying £260 a night for bed and breakfast accommodation and a prime vantage point.

Wartime memories flooded back when the RAF Battle of Britain

➤ Continued on page 21

AIR SHOW PAGES 20-27

DAILY ECHO

RED SKY

Arrows perform to crowd of 200,000

Picture: Pat Timmons ID: 7266604

By Paula Roberts
paula.roberts@bournemouthecho.co.uk

THEY'RE back.

The Red Arrows stormed into town yesterday in the first of three consecutive displays for the Bournemouth Air Festival.

The team performed a breathtaking display in front of more than 200,000 spectators who had lined the beach and cliff tops from Southbourne to West Cliff.

Hundreds of boats were anchored up in the bay between the two piers making an impressive sight, especially against the backdrop of RFA Mounts Bay.

The Red Arrows display began with a commemorative flypast with

➤ Continued on page 3

The MORE Bus Bournemouth

AIR FESTIVAL 2008
SATURDAY & SUNDAY, AUGUST 30 & 31

The **more** Bus
Bournemouth
AIR
Festival
™
Wilts & Dorset

www.bournemouthair.co.uk

DAILY ECHO
Official Souvenir Programme Sponsors

Bournemouth

SAVE 10% ON AIR FESTIVAL PICS!
See coupon inside or visit
bournemouthecho.co.uk
for full selection

DAILY ECHO

Monday, September 1, 2008   bournemouthecho.co.uk   38p

GREAT MEAL DEALS IN TASTE TODAY

SAIL TO FRANCE FROM ONLY £10! FERRY OFFER INSIDE (PER PERSON, MIN 2 PERSONS)

BACK IN 2009

HEADS UP: Residents of flats on the East Cliff get a startling view as the Red Arrows burst out of the town to start their display   Picture: Corin Messer   ID: 7272636

Air Festival even bigger next year!

WE'RE doing it again next year. And it will be even bigger and stay free of charge.

That was the pledge from council chiefs last night after Bournemouth's first air festival was voted a spectacular success.

The four-day event attracted more than three quarters of a million people and created a huge buzz as well as a major economic boost.

A crowd estimated at 380,000 packed the beaches and Overcliff on

Saturday alone – the town's busiest day on record.

Council leader Cllr Stephen Macloughlin told the Daily Echo: "It has been incredible and there's been the most amazing atmosphere day and night.

"We're going to do it in 2009 and if the support is there, we'll make it an annual event."

The dates for next year are Thursday, August 20 to Sunday, August 23.

See pages 3 and 20-27

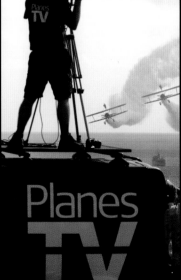

Planes
TV

2009

2009

A windswept sea greeted the guests heading to the RFA Mounts Bay ship for the launch event, which saw a Lynx helicopter lower a commando onto the deck and deliver a welcome letter to Navy chiefs.

The first night saw a record attempt – letting off 114,000 fireworks in one go in what was named Roar on the Shore. Around 100,000 people went down to the seafront to watch, but they were left disappointed when it was all over in, literally, a couple of seconds. It was something that was not to be repeated, but it failed to put a dampener on proceedings.

In the skies were the Blades, the Black Cats, Wingwalkers, Battle of Britain Memorial Flight, Yakovlevs, Red Bull Matadors, the Typhoon and, after 2008's disappointment, the mighty Vulcan.

The Red Arrows swooped in to provide the big highlight once more and display pilots were already talking about how the show had become a big favourite with them in only its second year. The drama continued on land, as the Royal Marine Commandos stormed the beach in a spectacular demonstration of their skills.

A flawless weekend saw organisers deliver on their promise to make the festival bigger and better, with an estimated 1.25 million people descending on the seafront, setting new records for the town. By the time the festival ended, the dates for 2010 had already been set, with hopes of another fantastic event.

OFFICIAL SOUVENIR PROGRAMME

DAILY ECHO

the more bus
Bournemouth
AIR
Festival
20th - 23rd August 2009
Wilts & Dorset

£5.00

Bournemouth
bournemouthair.co.uk

The Avro Vulcan is always one of the most appreciated visitors to the Air Festival. This Cold War bomber has a dedicated team of volunteers and fundraisers who work tirelessly to keep it flying.

The aircraft of the Battle of Britain Memorial Flight really need no introduction. The Lancaster, Spitfire and Hurricane have a place in the heart of all air festival goers. These historic planes are now based at RAF Coningsby.

The Russian Yakovlevs (far left) never cease to wow the crowds with their spectacular aerobatics; the Red Arrows (left) and the two Lynx helicopters of the Royal Navy's Black Cats, whose name is derived from the fierce feline on the 702 Naval Air Squadron emblem.

The crowds get up close and personal with the Royal Marines as they show what they can do, arriving by landing craft and storming the beach.

The Royal Marines display their crack skills, transferring from Lynx helicopter to fast boat as they head to the shore (far left) and Red Arrows, lights and smoke on.

The Sabre jet is an American aircraft which played a pivotal role in the Korean War by winning back air superiority for the Allied cause.

The two aircraft of the Guinot Wingwalkers almost seem to be touching as they perform their spectacular routines over the sea.

Colourful, courageous, unique. That's how the RAF Falcons characterise their displays and it's hard to disagree when you watch these highly-skilled, high-trained, parachutists touch down with pinpoint accuracy.

Is it art? A demonstration of gymnastics, with performer suspended beneath a balloon, draws an appreciative crowd in the Lower Gardens.

The night time activities have proved hugely popular, especially the spectacular balloon glow (left) and the fireworks (centre). Meanwhile, with their feet firmly on the ground (sometimes), the Royal Marines Combat Display Team show why you wouldn't mess with them.

Two big beasts... The Avro Vulcan (above), one of the most iconic of British aircraft which delights crowds wherever it goes and the distinctive B17 Flying Fortress (below), a familiar sight in southern England during the Second World War.

The Chinook is just as recognisable as the two aircraft opposite. This twin-rotored giant is a mainstay of both the US and UK armed forces.

The Chinook shows off its versatility over the Bournemouth skies, performing moves that seem to defy its size and shape. One of the Yaks goes into a roll (far right).

The Avro Lancaster flies in majestically with the Isle of Wight as its backdrop (far left), the Sabre (above left) and the Guinot Wingwalkers (left) go through their paces, while the RAF King Air takes a more leisurely approach (above).

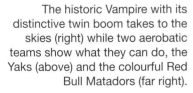

The historic Vampire with its distinctive twin boom takes to the skies (right) while two aerobatic teams show what they can do, the Yaks (above) and the colourful Red Bull Matadors (far right).

With its deafening roar and the reheat of its engines, the Typhoon goes through its unique routine (above) while spectators look as though they're having a close shave with the Red Arrows – but it's only a poster (right). The Blades (far right) show just how sharp they are.

The Red Bull Matadors go through their paces (left, above and below) while two of the Red Arrows pass within feet of each other in front of the shoreline (right). The Blades soar into the blue skies (far right).

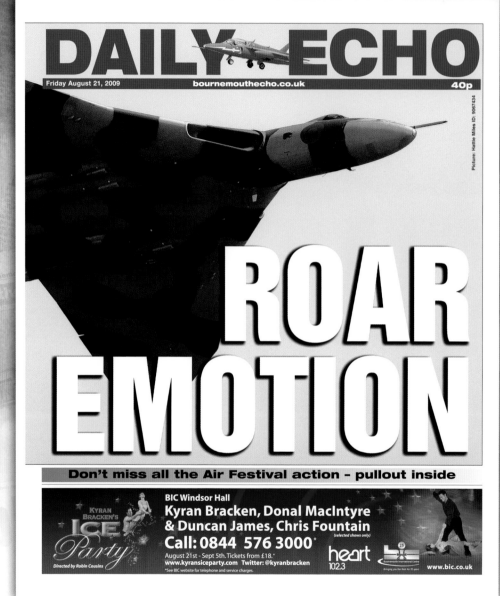

DAILY ECHO

Saturday August 22 2009 · bournemouthecho.co.uk · 60p

Picture: Corin Messer ID: 9072848

RED HOT!

The Arrows and more air festival action – pullout inside

AIR FEST 09

bournemouthecho.co.uk · MONDAY AUGUST 24 2009 **DAILY ECHO**

Bournemouth **AIR** Festival
20th - 23rd August 2009

AIRSIDE BY THE SEASIDE: EIGHT PAGES OF PICTURES FROM DAYS THREE AND FOUR OF THE SHOW

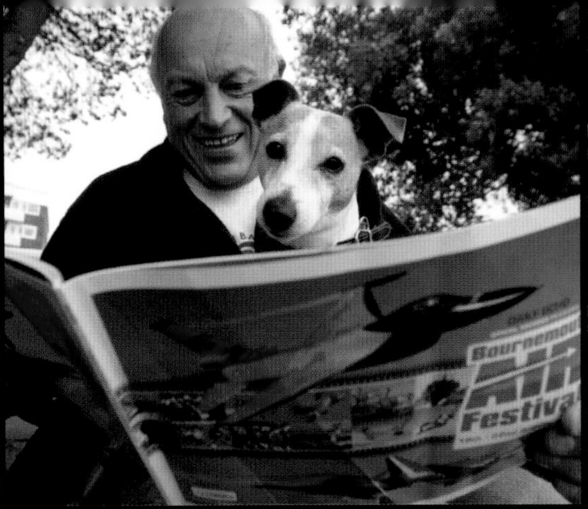

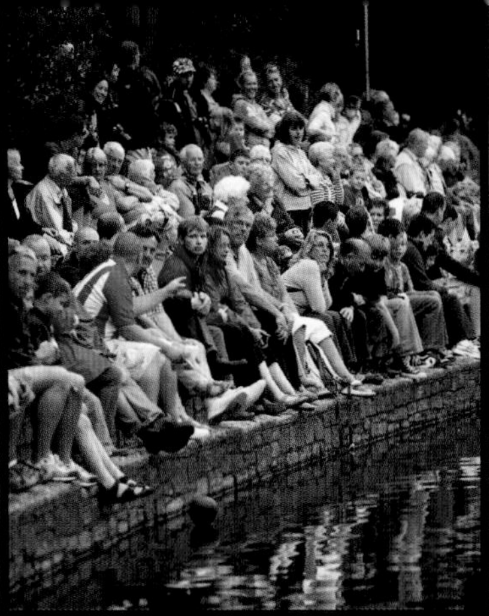

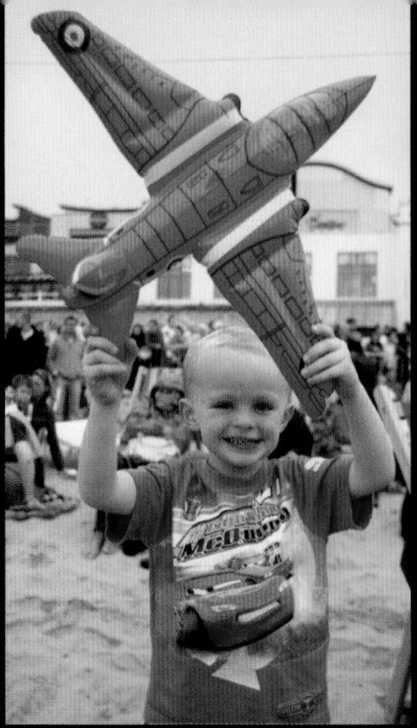

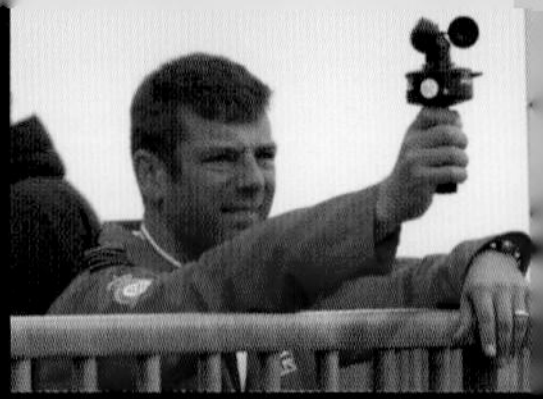

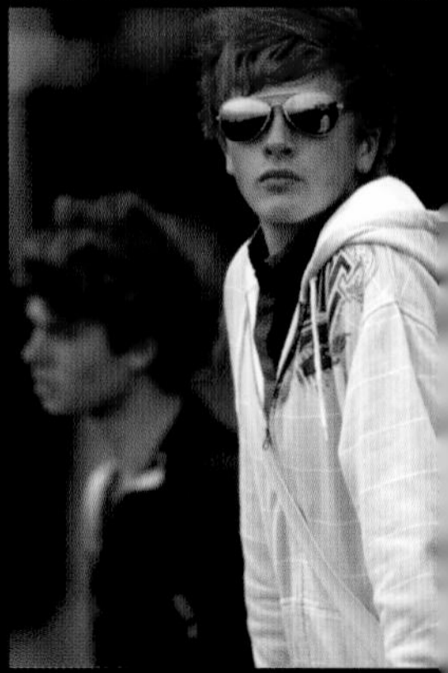

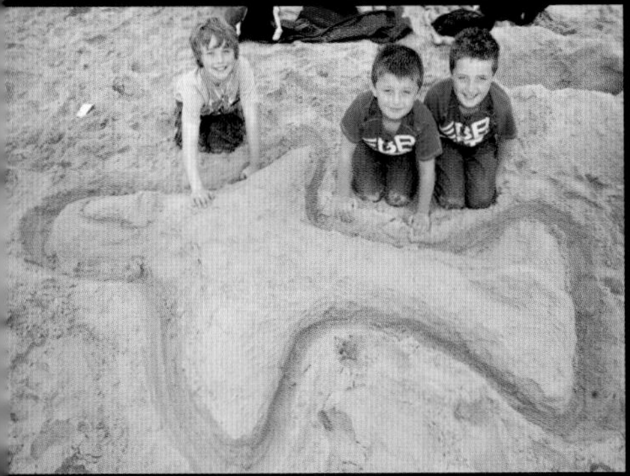

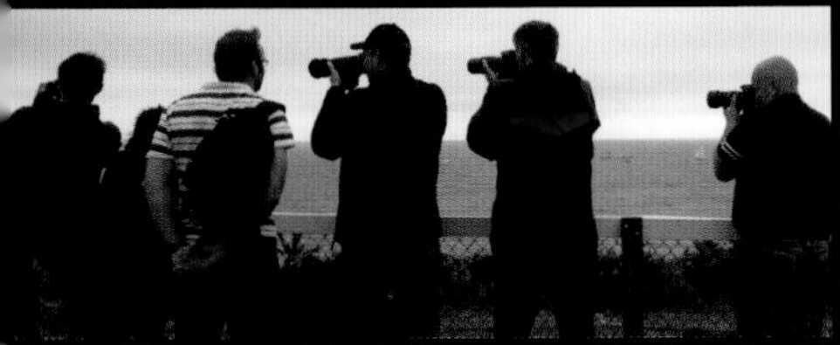

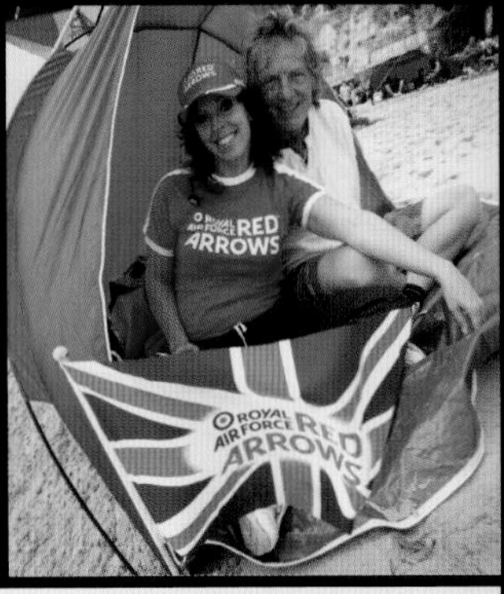
ROYAL AIR FORCE RED ARROWS

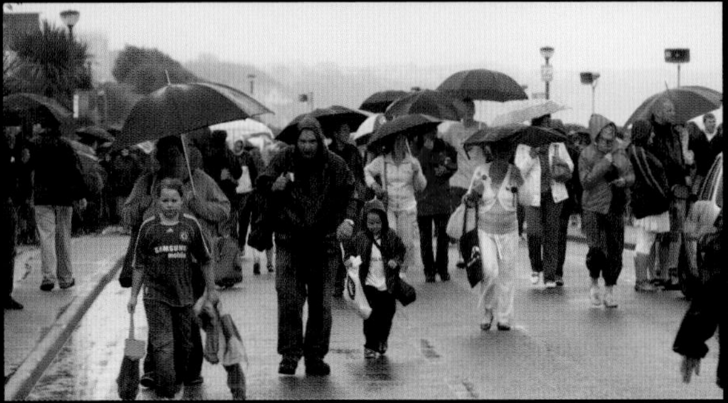

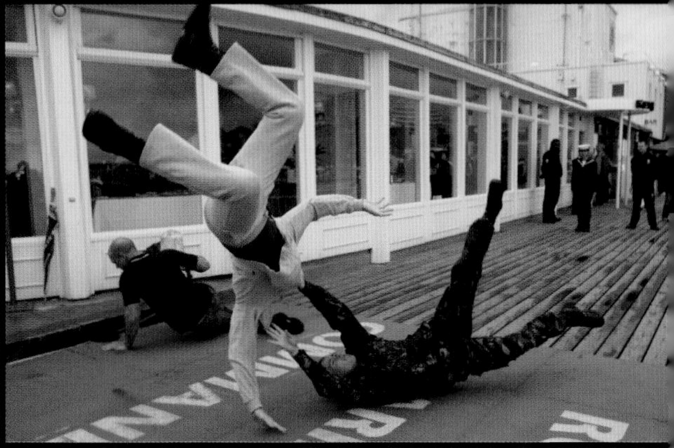

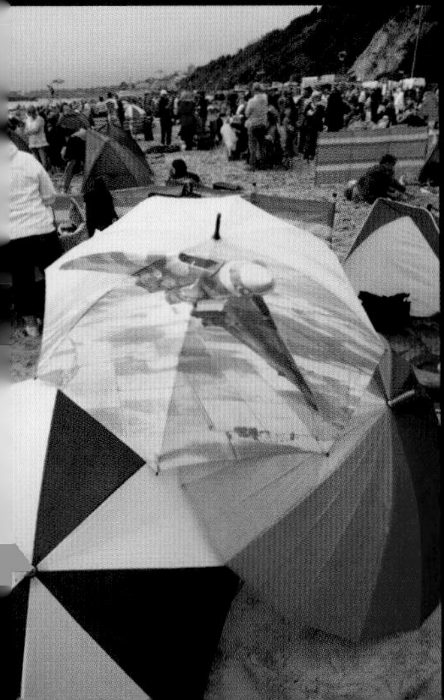

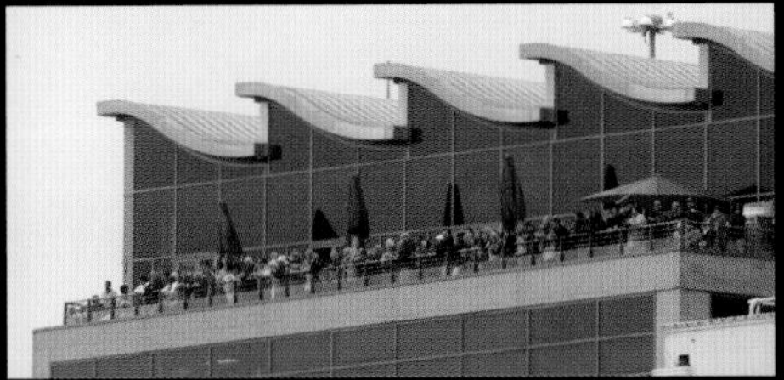

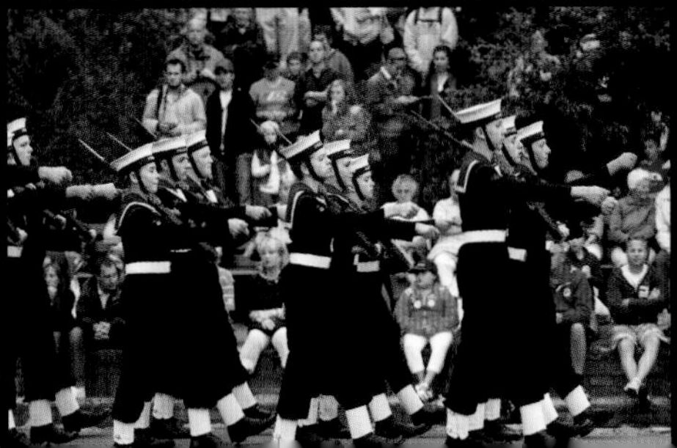

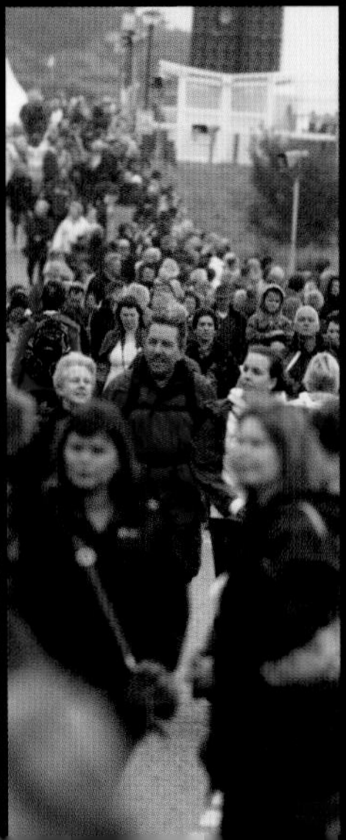

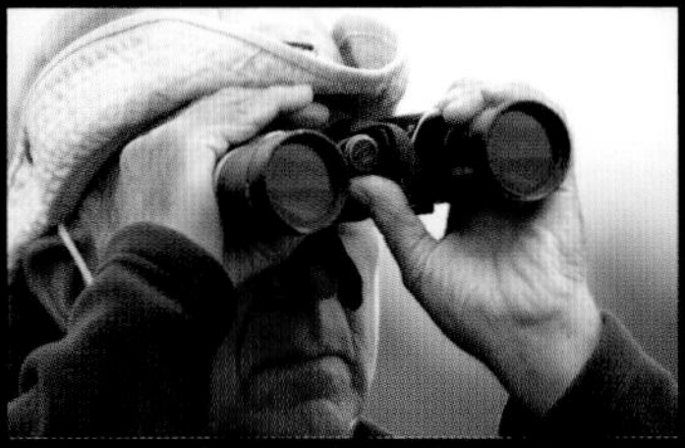

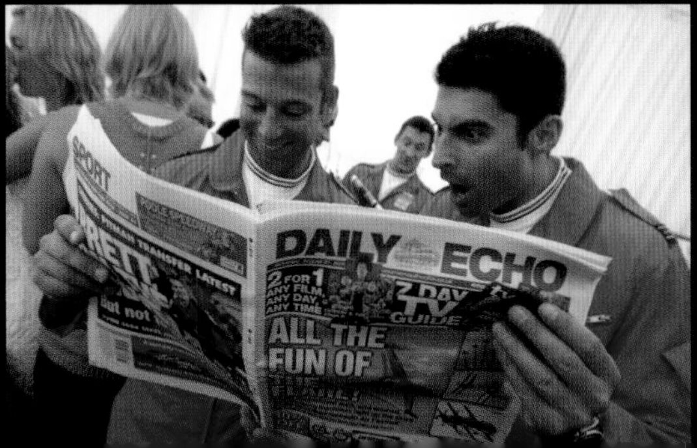
DAILY ECHO
ALL THE FUN OF

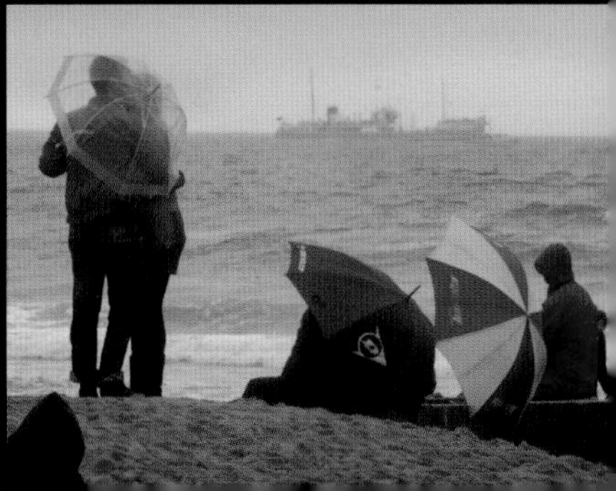

2010

2010

The third event kicked off in style, with another dramatic launch event, this time on the pier. Rather than being winched in, a Royal Marine had to battle his way past the 'enemy' to deliver his letter to Navy chiefs. And the show got Royal approval, with the Queen sending a note of good wishes as Bournemouth celebrated its 200th anniversary.

The first day saw early drizzle disappear in time for the flying to begin, with the Wingwalkers – showing off new colours – providing one of the big highlights.

New for this year was the boom of the Dutch F-16 fighter jet, which proved a big favourite with the crowds, as did the colourful Miss Demeanour Hunter jet. And for the first time dusk displays were added to the line-up.

The Red Arrows roared in once again with precision timing, and the Battle of Britain Memorial Flight marked the 70th anniversary of the Battle of Britain in an emotional display.

Organisers faced their first real challenges as the weather caused problems, with low cloud and high winds curtailing displays, particularly on the Saturday and Sunday of the show. Rain and cloud played havoc with the flying programme on the two days, but it failed to dampen spirits and the dates were confirmed for 2011 and beyond.

Fans of fast jets were not disappointed, with the Typhoon (above) and Dutch F-16 (right) both making roaring appearances over the seafront, while the Lancaster from the Battle of Britain Memorial Flight (far right) brought a touch of history to the proceedings.

The Spitfire from the Battle of Britain Memorial Flight and
The Tigers both brought a patriotic note to the Air Festival.

The Pitts Duo look too close for comfort during their daring display of aerobatics, with smoke trailing behind.

The Tucano (above) shows part of the training that all pilots go through before they end up on fast jets like the Typhoon (right), while the Dutch F-16 (far right) adds more speed and power to the show.

Festival favourite the Vulcan arrives at Bournemouth Airport for the event, giving our photographer a chance to get an up-close view of the Cold War bomber.

Stunning formation flying from The Blades (below), while the Black Cats helicopter team (right) shows off its moves.

There was plenty of drama during the Royal Marines beach assault, while back in the skies the crowds got the chance to see the Hawk (below) show off what it could do, along with (far right), gravity-defying aerobatics from the CAP232.

As always there was plenty to see and do on the ground as well as in the air, with drama in the form of the Royal Marines beach assault (far right), as well as pomp and ceremony from RM Band Collingwood. The Royal Marines Combat Display Team demonstrated some close-quarters conflict in the Gardens (left).

One of the highlights of the year's show, the colourful Dutch Royal Air Force F-16 lit up the sky. It managed to fly even when other aircraft were grounded by the weather. Its colossal speed and noise made it a big favourite with festival-goers.

The F-16 (above and below) dazzled the crowds with its smoke and flares, while the Vulcan (right) put a smile on everyone's faces by making a surprise fly-past after the scheduled flying displays had finished.

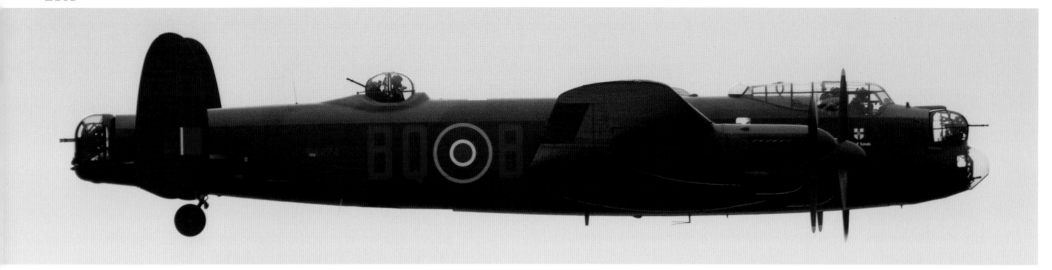

The Battle of Britain Memorial Flight brought a sense of history to the occasion, with the Lancaster (above) and Spitfire (right) gracefully showing their capabilities and paying tribute to those who flew in them during the Battle of Britain and the rest of World War Two.

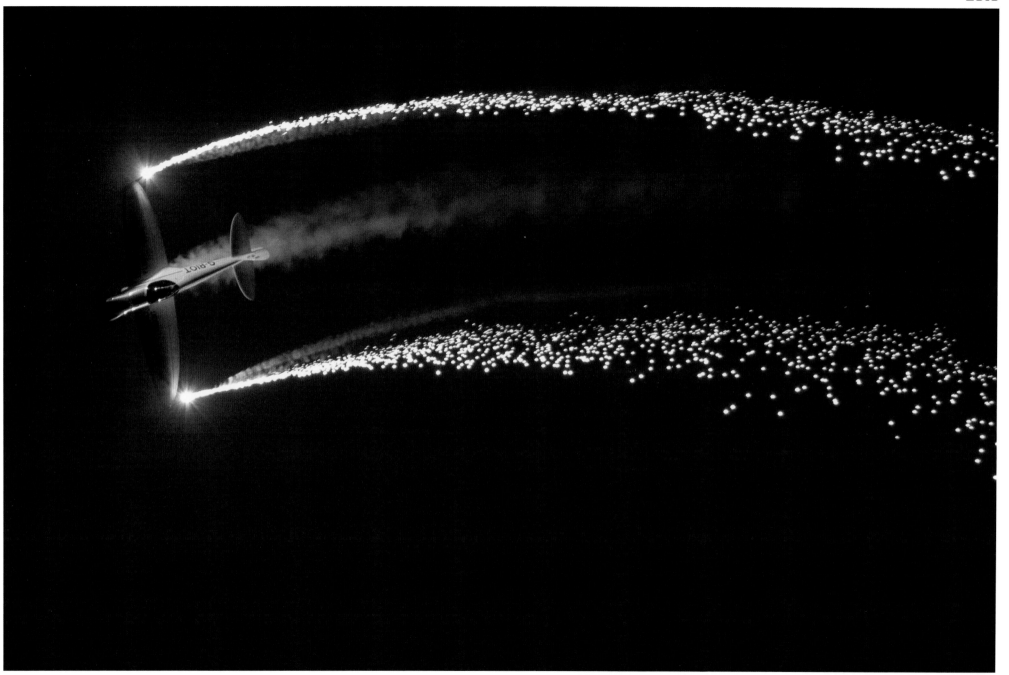

By dusk, a moving and colourful display with wingtip fireworks and smoke trails.

The Breitling Wingwalkers are always a hit with the festival crowds. It takes a special kind of daring to perform gymnastics while strapped to the front of a biplane and the girls on the team save their best for last, leaving their harnesses at the end of the routine to sit on the wing. Meanwhile (far right) the Red Arrows roared into view, bringing some colour to the dull skies.

The Red Bull Matadors (left) showed off their precision aerobatic skills, twisting and turning in all directions, while the Miss Demeanour Hunter Jet (below), brought speed, power and noise to the proceedings – not to mention a lot of colour. Pictured right, the Wingwalkers show off their skills.

The Dutch F-16 fighter jet (left) was a big hit with the crowds, while the Lancaster bomber (above) made for a great picture as it came into view with the Isle of Wight in the background. The Blades (right), show some seriously close flying.

It's not just about the planes, as the Royal Navy's Black Cats (right) proved when they showed the versatility and sometimes gravity-defying capabilities of their Lynx helicopters. The Navy continued to muscle in on the show when the Sea King (far right) dropped in, while the RAF showed off their flying skills with their flagship team, the Red Arrows (below).

The Dutch F-16 lights up its afterburner as it fires up the crowds (above, top left and left) with plenty of smoke in evidence as it shows off everything it can do – including flying upside down (right). At the other end of the scale, a glider lights up the night sky during the dusk displays with wingtip fireworks.

The magnificent Vulcan lands at Bournemouth Airport with parachute deployed to help it slow down.

2011

2011

If 2010 showed the impact the weather could have on the event, nobody was expecting what 2011 would bring. Flash floods hit the first day of the show – with the gardens flooded in minutes. Needless to say there was no flying on day one as torrential rain bombarded the town.

But it was a flash and no more and the sun came out on day two, as things got firmly back on track when the Red Arrows flew into view. The chaotic weather of 24 hours earlier became a distant memory as fans enjoyed highlights that included a new sight – the Merlin helicopter – alongside the BBMF and crazy aerobatics from Gerald Cooper.

Also wowing the crowds were the incredible pair of Tornado jets – displaying for the first time – along with the Wingwalkers, The Blades and Miss Demeanour. The Commandos stormed the beach and the Night Air displays were even more spectacular than the year before. But, with the festival firmly back on track, tragedy struck on the Saturday.

After the usual perfect display from the Red Arrows, Flt Lt Jon Egging was killed when his jet crashed as it returned to Bournemouth Airport. It left the town in total shock and Sunday saw a huge outpouring of tributes.

In true British spirit, the show went on, with the final day an emotional one for all.

An unusual combination as the historic Spitfire joins the aerobatic RV8tors over Bournemouth seafront (above), while (right), eyes weren't always on the skies as the spectacular balloon glow took place on the beach as the sun went down.

The first day of the festival was a washout as freak storms hit Bournemouth, but the Sea King helicopter (above) managed to take part in a scaled-down launch event. When the sun came back this fan (right) displayed his allegiance to the RAF, while the Wingwalkers (far right) showed their skills over the Royal Navy ships anchored in the bay.

The Red Arrows break (above) and the sedate King Air (below).

Royal Navy and Royal Air Force both showed off what they could do, with the Merlin (far left) helicopter demonstrating its capabilities, while the solo Hawk display (left) gave crowds a close-up view of the Red Arrows' jet of choice. The range of aircraft was evident with nostalgia from the Battle of Britain Memorial Flight (below) and cutting-edge jet action with the ear-splitting Tornado.

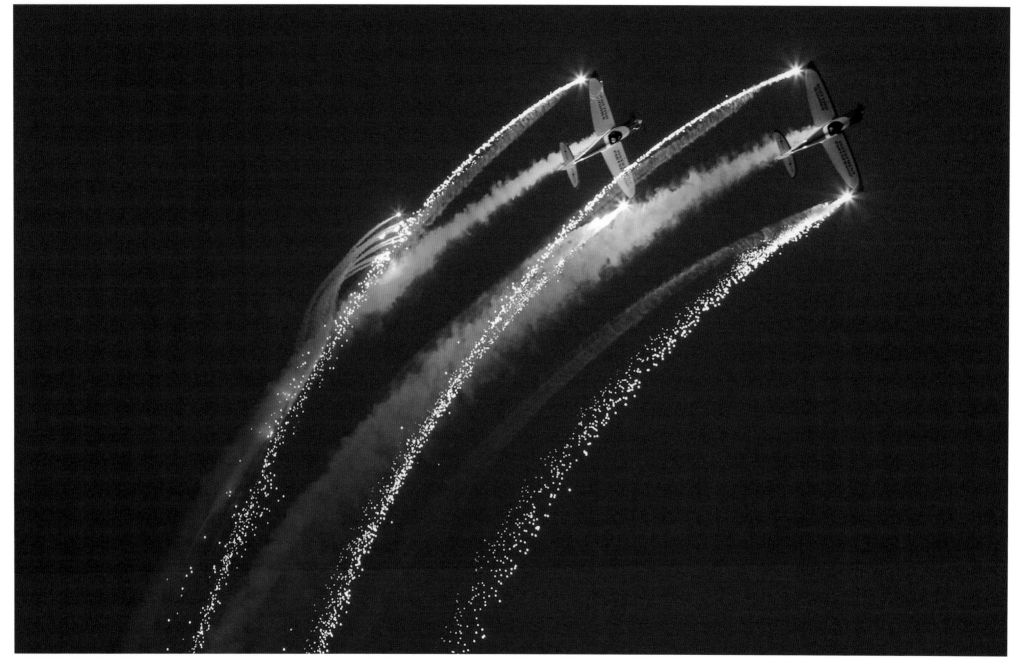

The SWIP Team Twister Duo brought the displays to a graceful and reflective close as the sun went down, with their pyrotechnic-laden display set to backing music (above). The Navy's Merlin helicopter (far right) demonstrated winching a man from the sea and the Spitfire (right) showed off its stunning lines.

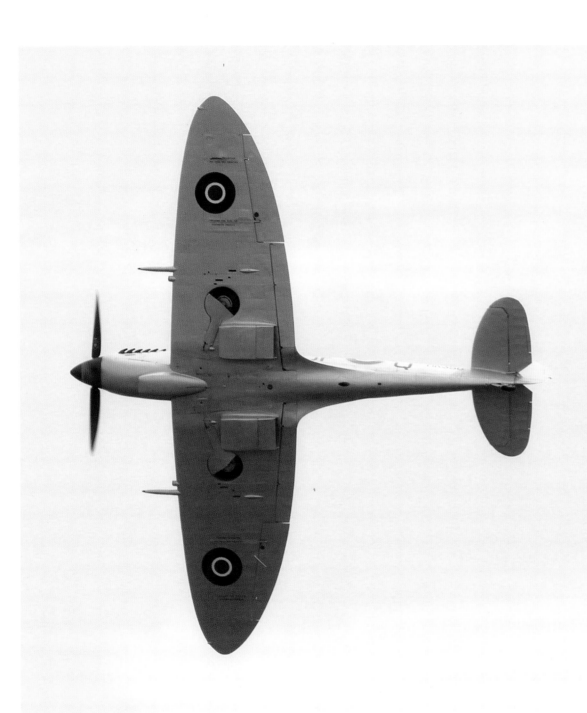

American Flying Fortress Sally B, which appeared in the film Memphis Belle (above), offered the crowds the chance to see Europe's last airworthy example of the B-17 WW2 bomber in flight. For those who enjoy speed and close-flying thrills, Miss Demeanour (far left) and the Blades (left) had them in abundance.

There was drama on the beach as the Royal Marines staged an assault, showing why they are among the best in the world. They demonstrated their capabilities on sea, land and air in dramatic fashion as the crowds looked on.

As the sun shone the flash floods that wiped out the first day of the event were a distant memory and the Wingwalkers made the most of it to perform in front of clear blue skies. The Royal Air Force's Tucano (bottom middle) is another rung on the ladder that all pilots have to go through on their way to qualifying.

A big treat for fans came in the form of the Bournemouth-based Sea Vixen. A real piece of Royal Navy heritage, it gave a demonstration of its capabilities and design over the seafront.

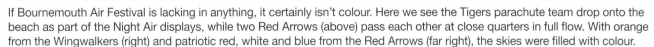

If Bournemouth Air Festival is lacking in anything, it certainly isn't colour. Here we see the Tigers parachute team drop onto the beach as part of the Night Air displays, while two Red Arrows (above) pass each other at close quarters in full flow. With orange from the Wingwalkers (right) and patriotic red, white and blue from the Red Arrows (far right), the skies were filled with colour.

Here are the stars of the show – the mighty Red Arrows. Flying in over the cliff top with split second precision, the Diamond Nine dazzled the crowds at every turn with their flawless flying. Pulling off passes with what appeared to be inches between them, flying at every conceivable angle and filling the sky with colour and smoke, the biggest crowds on the beach were reserved for the pride of the nation.

The magnificent Red Arrows in different formations.

The Red Arrows show why they are the stars of the show.

As the Festival got back on track after the wash-out first day, tragedy struck. Having completed another flawless show over the seafront, Red 4, Flt Lt Jon Egging, crashed as the team returned to Bournemouth Airport. His jet came down near Throop on the Saturday afternoon of the event and the news was greeted with shock as it filtered back to the town. It triggered an outpouring of emotion and tributes. Flags flew at half mast and masses of flowers were left at the Town Hall, but organisers vowed that the final day of the show would go ahead.

Night Air encouraged many fans to stay on the seafront until the end of the evening, with the SWIP duo bringing proceedings to a close with a calm and graceful display involving dazzling pyrotechnics. Earlier the Hawk (below), most famous as the jet used by the Red Arrows, went solo.

Jet power was in abundance, with the mighty Tornado GR4 (above) ripping through the skies, while Bournemouth enjoyed a display not seen anywhere else – the striking Miss Demeanour Hunter Jet displaying in tandem with the Sea Vixen (below). With both restored at Bournemouth, it was a real treat for fans on the beach and cliff tops.

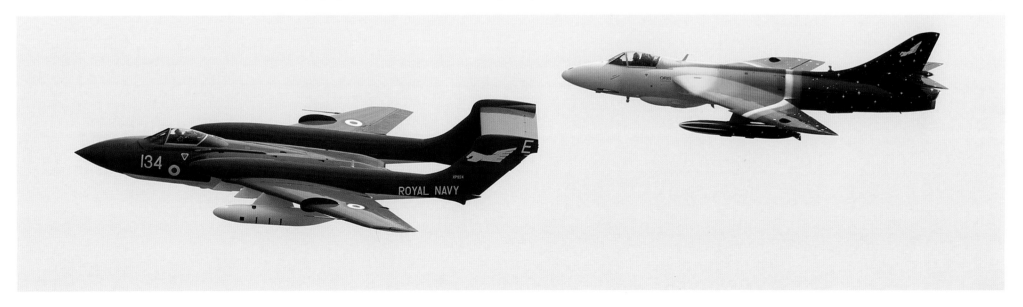

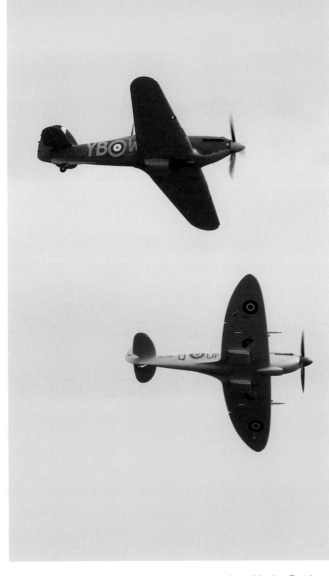

Historic flying was not in short supply, with the Battle of Britain's Memorial flight making for a great picture as it took a solo flight over the beach (left and right), while (above) the Hurricane and Spitfire later joined in to show why both aircraft were so vital to the outcome of World War Two.

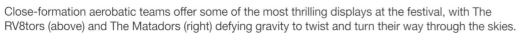

Close-formation aerobatic teams offer some of the most thrilling displays at the festival, with The RV8tors (above) and The Matadors (right) defying gravity to twist and turn their way through the skies.

The dual display from the Miss Demeanour Hunter Jet and the Sea Vixen was historic and unique to the town, with it being the only place that the pair flew together – a real treat for enthusiasts.

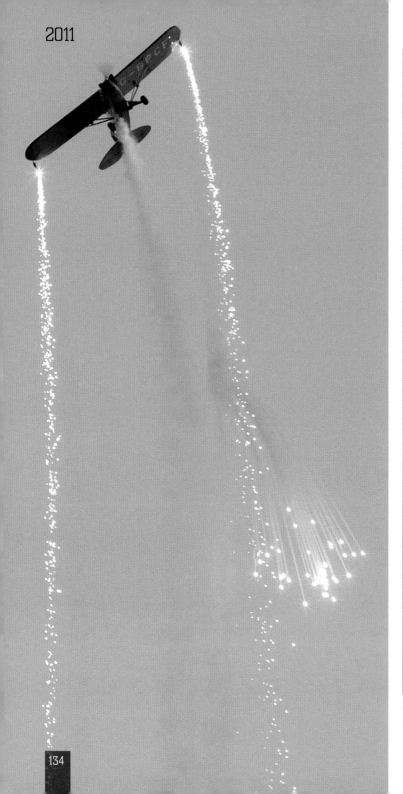

More dazzling fireworks from the SWIP Team (above) as dusk falls over the seafront, while O'Brien's Flying Circus (left) adds a bit of old fashioned crazy flying and some fireworks of its own.

Crowds were able to enjoy a solo display from the Spitfire, giving them a chance to appreciate its swooping lines and distinctive throaty roar.

Bournemouth will always be an emotional place for the Red Arrows after the tragic events of 2011. Here we see a simple but poignant tribute left at the town hall in memory of Flt Lt Jon Egging – known as Eggman – who died when his Hawk jet crashed near Throop as the team returned to Bournemouth Airport.

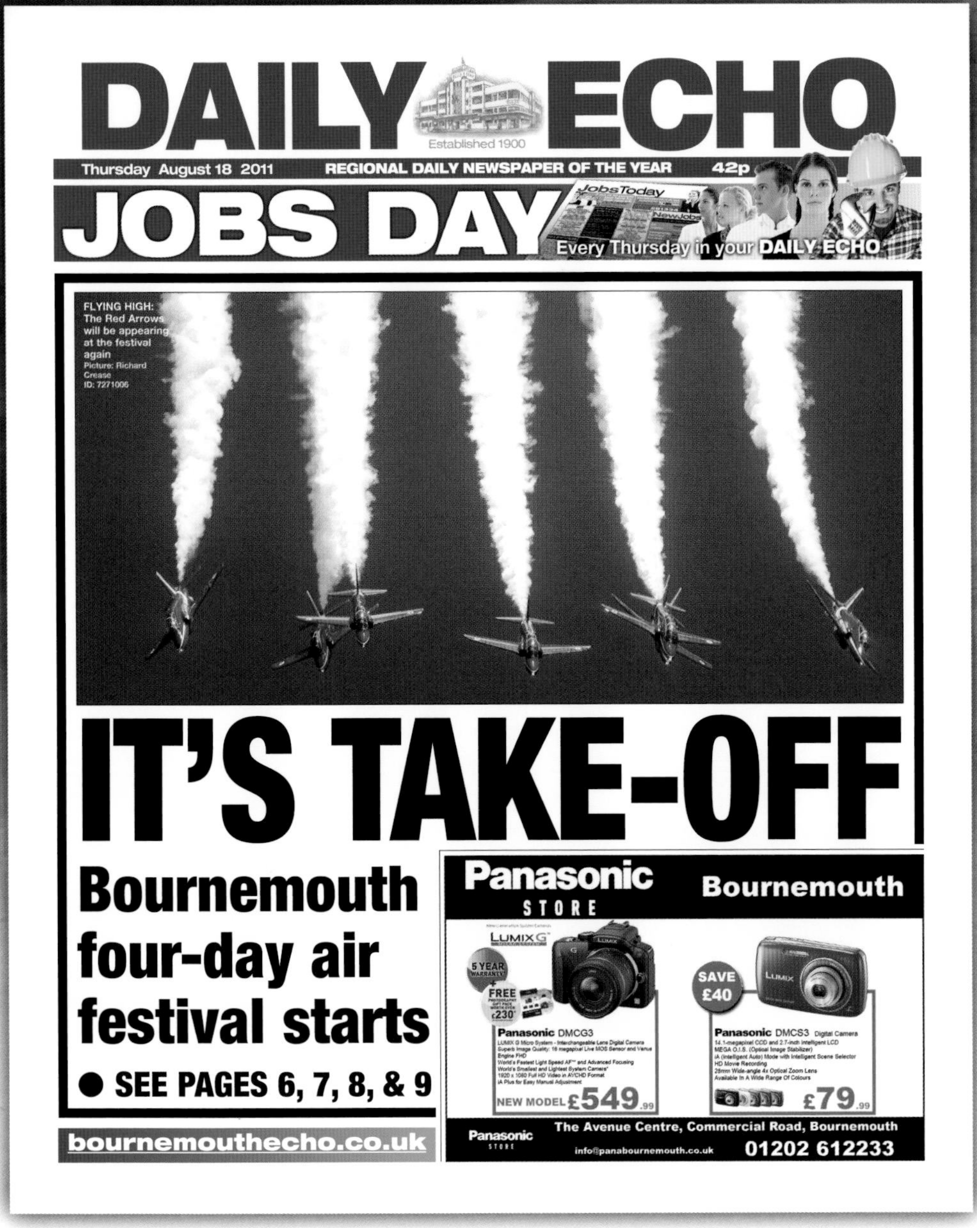

DAILY ECHO

Established 1900

Thursday August 18 2011 REGIONAL DAILY NEWSPAPER OF THE YEAR 42p

JOBS DAY Every Thursday in your DAILY ECHO

FLYING HIGH: The Red Arrows will be appearing at the festival again Picture: Richard Crease ID: 7271006

IT'S TAKE-OFF

Bournemouth four-day air festival starts

● SEE PAGES 6, 7, 8, & 9

bournemouthecho.co.uk

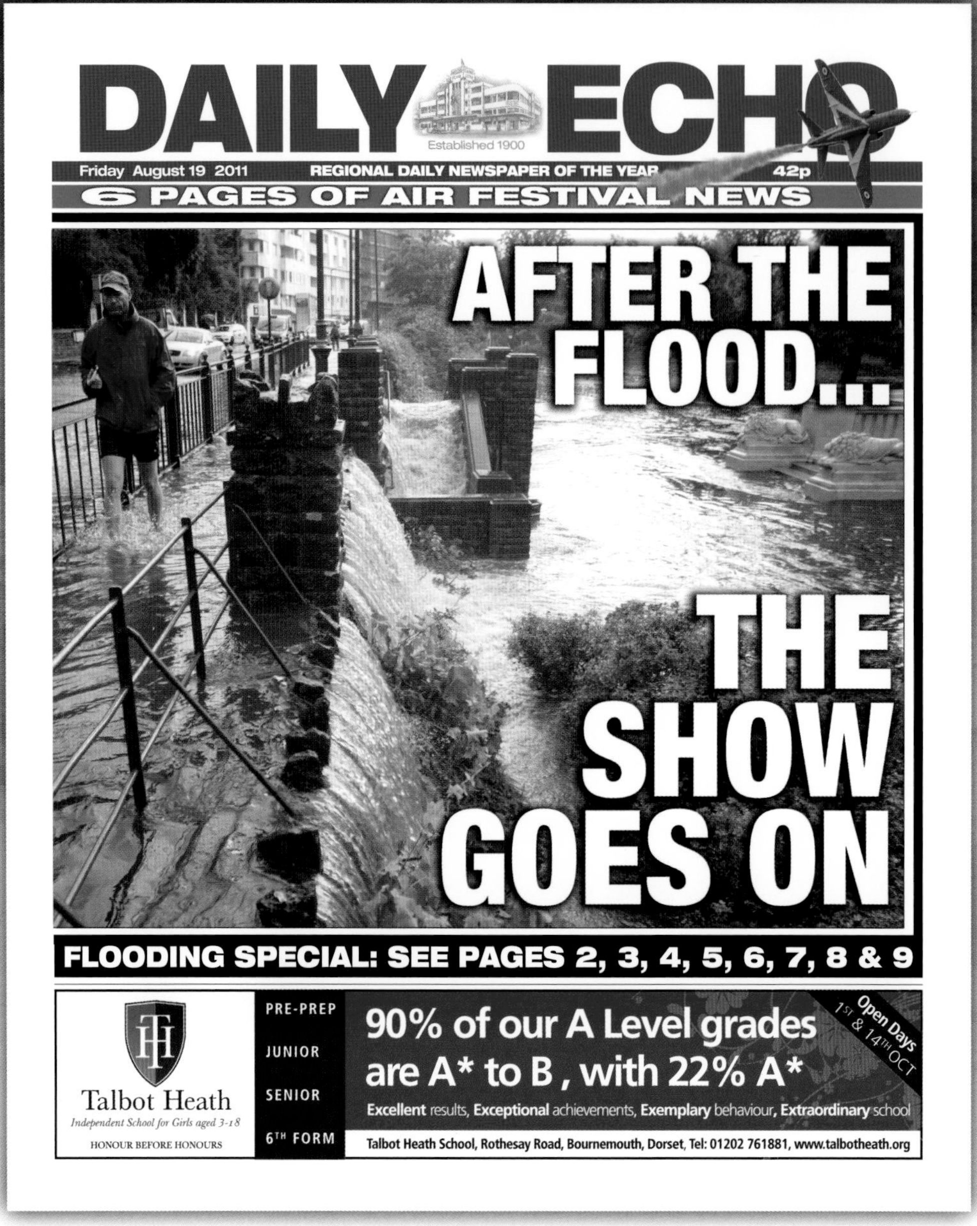

DAILY ECHO

Established 1900

Friday August 19 2011 REGIONAL DAILY NEWSPAPER OF THE YEAR 42p

6 PAGES OF AIR FESTIVAL NEWS

AFTER THE FLOOD...

THE SHOW GOES ON

FLOODING SPECIAL: SEE PAGES 2, 3, 4, 5, 6, 7, 8 & 9

DAILY ECHO

Established 1900

Saturday August 20 2011 · REGIONAL DAILY NEWSPAPER OF THE YEAR · 65p

Thousands see Bournemouth air festival soaring again

FESTIVAL FAVOURITES: The Red Arrows thrill the crowd
Picture: Richard Crease

FLYING HIGH

PICTURE SPECIAL: PAGES 10, 11, 12, 13, 14, 15, 16 & 17

DAILY ECHO

Established 1900

Monday August 22 2011 · REGIONAL DAILY NEWSPAPER OF THE YEAR · 42p

TRIBUTES PAID TO HERO PILOT

RED MISSED: Flt Lt Jon Egging at Bournemouth Airport Picture: Mike Boss

ROYAL AIR

● FULL STORY: PAGES 2-8 ● AIR FESTIVAL: PAGES 9-13

2012

The Red Arrows were back in Bournemouth for what was an emotional time for everybody following the events of 2011.

A sculpture in memory of Jon Egging was unveiled on the East Overcliff ahead of the event, and the team's display included a tribute to him, as well as Flt Lt Sean Cunningham, who was killed in November 2011 in an accident on the ground at the team's home base. A fundraising ball saw Jon's widow, Emma, in town.

Once more the crowds were treated to fantastic flying by day and night, with the Vulcan making its return and the Tigers parachute team in a typically-patriotic show. Hundreds of thousands of people flocked to the beach and enjoyed the thrill of two Tornado jets and a historic re-enactment, while favourites including the Wingwalkers, Miss Demeanour, The Blades and the Chinook all took to the skies.

After the weather problems of the previous two years, a near-full display programme was delivered and estimates again put visitor numbers at around one million.

On the ground the attractions expanded with a new music stage put up at Boscombe – artists included Rizzle Kicks, Newton Faulkner and Scouting for Girls.

After five events, Bournemouth Air Festival continued to go from strength-to-strength.

The Blades show off their close-quarters daring flying complete with smoke trails over the sea.

The crowds were treated to not one but two Tornado jets, here showing their afterburners as they roar over the seafront.

The Tornado shows its undercarriage as it manoeuvres over the seafront, giving the crowds a view of its armaments and a glimpse of its red-hot afterburners.

The Tornados were a big hit with the crowds, showing what they are capable of in their front line roles including the war in Afghanistan.

The Tigers (left and above) dropped onto the seafront in patriotic fashion, landing on the beach complete with flares. British and American historic flying action (right) was on show as part of a re-enactment, with the Spitfire and the P51 Mustang in action.

The RAF Hawk (above and right) was decked out in red, white and blue for its 2012 display. The Red Arrow's jet of choice took to the skies on its own to give crowds a closer view of its capabilities. Meanwhile the Army Lynx (below) showed what it could do.

The action moves from the skies to the sea and beach as the Royal Marines stage an assault, taking on the 'enemy' and securing the beach. In a dramatic raid, they storm the beach in a landing craft and a blaze of mock gunfire.

King Air (left) gives a demonstration of what pilots have to go through as part of their training, while O'Brien's Flying Circus (right) delivers some fun flying with fireworks as dusk falls.

The Tucano enjoys some blue skies and shows why it is such a key part of the training that all RAF pilots have to go through.

The historic Venom's unusual design captivates the crowds (above), while this stunning picture of The Blades shows formation flying at its best.

The colourful Miss Demeanour Hunter Jet (above) roared across the seafront, this year with former Red Arrows leader Ben Murphy in the cockpit. Despite zooming across the beach at high speed in a blaze of colour and noise, Ben still finds time to do a slow flypast – waving from the cockpit as he does. The King Air (right).

The Vulcan (left) has had an eventful history at Bournemouth, with bad weather and technical problems sometimes keeping it on the ground. But it flies in 2012 and is a big hit as always. Another big draw, is the Chinook, with its distinctive sounds.
It shows what it does on operations, pulling turns and angles that don't seem possible for such a machine.

The Catalina (below), P51 Mustang and Spitfire (above) all took part in a historic re-enactment, based on a daring rescue from the sea during World War Two.

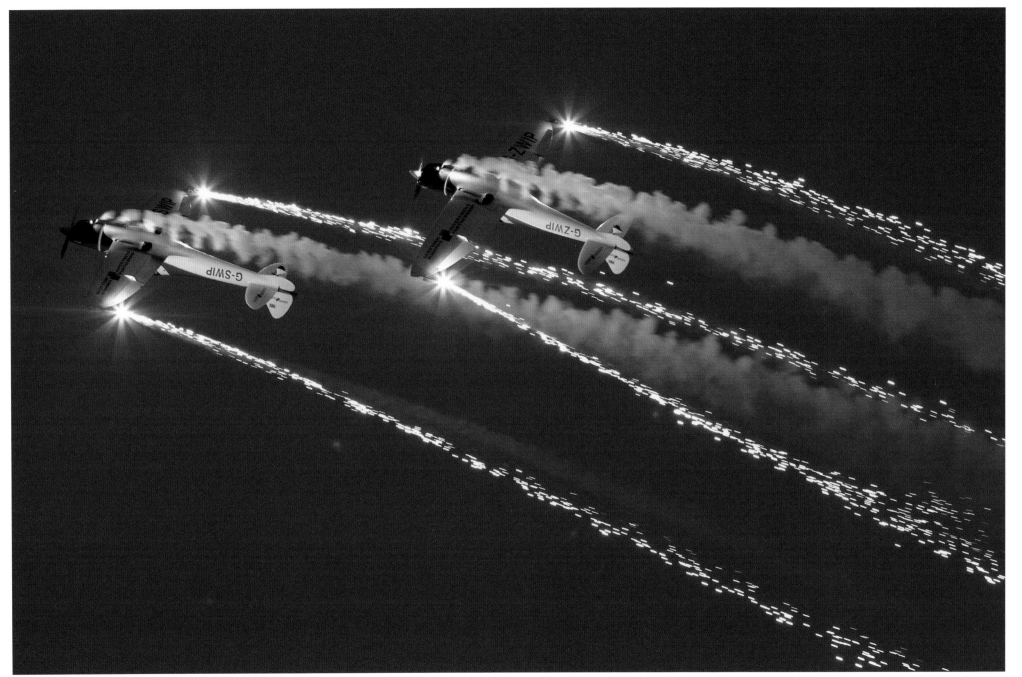

A spectacular shot of the SWIP Team, lighting up the sky during the dusk Night Air displays.

The Black Cats helicopter display team has always been popular at the Air Festival and here they show why. Close-quarters formation flying – going forwards, backwards and up and down – displays the versatility of the Royal Navy's Lynx aircraft.

Stunning pictures show the variety of displays on offer with (top) an incredible image of the Wingwalkers seemingly too close for comfort, while the SWIP Team (right) dazzle as they display against the night sky. The Merlin helicopter (above) appeared over the sea, while (far right) this colourful shot shows just how brave the Wingwalking girls are.

It was an emotional year for the Red Arrows and the crowds who came to watch them. With Britain in the spirit of the Olympics and the Diamond Jubilee, they showed why they are the pride of the country with their patriotic display. The team is pictured (far right) passing over the memorial on the East Cliff in memory of Flt Lt Jon Egging, who died following the previous year's display at Bournemouth.

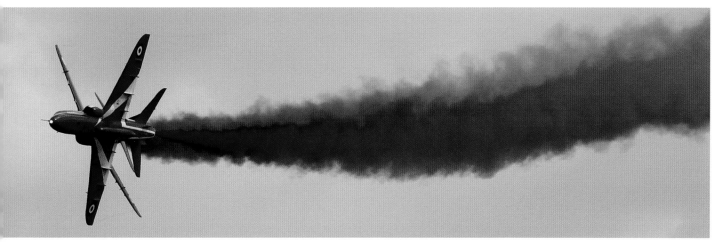

Stunning pictures of a stunning team in action. The Red Arrows perform a flypast in tribute of lost colleagues, showing red and white smoke as they pass near the Jon Egging memorial. The display also included the renowned daring flying (left) and (right) this beautiful picture shows the seven strong team in perfect union with red, white and blue smoke trailing against the sky.

The Red Arrows (above) show why they are the best in the world, while the epic Tornado (right) demonstrates its speed as a cloud of water vapour flashes over its wings.

DAILY ECHO

Thursday August 30 2012   bournemouthecho.co.uk   45p

FULL STEAM AHEAD
Dorset's Great Fair begins: Page 9

HALF PRICE ENTRY
AT SEA LIFE PARK! Turn to page 22

JUDITH CARRIES THE PARALYMPIC TORCH
Page 7

UP AND AWAY

Red Arrows kick off Air Festival today:
Pages 3,4&5 plus free poster inside

DAILY ECHO

Saturday September 1, 2012   bournemouthecho.co.uk   65p

FLYING HIGH

PAGES 2,3,4,5,6&7 PLUS FREE POSTER

AND FIVE YEARS OF THE AIR FESTIVAL 16-PAGE SOUVENIR PULLOUT INSIDE

The beautiful lines of the Spitfire grace a colourful sky.

who did what

Designed by: **Neil Keeping**

Cover: **John Nesbitt**

Cover photograph: **Richard Crease**

Editing by: **Toby Granville, Andy Martin and Steven Smith**

Pictures: **Richard Crease, Corin Messer, Sally Adams, Jon Beal, Michelle Luther, Hattie Miles, Pat Timmons, Rob Fleming, Gary Ellson, Samantha Cook, Mark Hinwood.**

Picture research: **Michelle Luther**

Sales: **Marie Burnett**

Published by:

DAILY ECHO

bournemouthecho.co.uk

DorsetECHO

dorsetecho.co.uk

© Newsquest Media (Southern) Ltd
ISBN: 978-0-9570634-3-3

Printed by: Westdale Press Limited, 70 Portmanmoor Road Industrial Estate, East Moors, Cardiff, CF24 5HB. Tel: 029 2066 2600

In association with

Castle Cameras
329 Wimborne Road
Winton
Bournemouth
BH9 2AD
01202 526606
www.castlecameras.co.uk